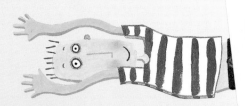

Focus ENGLISH

Anthology
Text extracts
3

Written and compiled by
Chris Buckton and **Pie Corbett**

Series Editor: **Leonie Bennett**

Heinemann

Heinemann Educational Publishers
Halley Court, Jordan Hill, Oxford OX2 8EJ
a division of Reed Educational & Professional Publishing Limited

Heinemann is a registered trademark of Reed Educational & Professional Publishing Limited

OXFORD MELBOURNE AUCKLAND
JOHANNESBURG BLANTYRE IBADAN GABORONE
PORTSMOUTH NH (USA) CHICAGO

© Reed Educational and Professional Publishing Ltd, 1999

The moral right of the proprietor has been asserted.

First published 1999

03 02 01 00 99
10 9 8 7 6 5 4 3 2 1

British Library Cataloguing in Publication Data
A catalogue record for this book is available from the British Library.

ISBN 0 435 10678 3   single copy
ISBN 0 435 10642 2   6 copy pack

All rights reserved. No part of this publication may be reproduced or transmitted
in any form, or by any means, electronic or mechanical, including photocopying,
recording or any information storage and retrieval system without permission
in writing from the publishers.

Designed by Celia Floyd and Susan Clarke
Colour repro by Ambassador Litho
Printed in Spain

Contents

Goosey Farm

We'd come from a little terraced house in a city to Goosey Farm with its two staircases and rooms that went on for ever and ever so you could never finish exploring. There were beams in the ceilings and panelling on the walls and a fireplace as wide as a gate with a wooden seat built into it.

Tiny windows sat in walls as wide as your outstretched arms, while the back of the house
10 crouched under a steep hill that sheltered Goosey from the winds and the winter snows.

Gene Kemp

Cotter's Yard was a maze of twisted rusting wrecks. The muddy tracks through it were littered with car tyres. Great piles of cars towered all about him now as he picked his way round the potholes. And all the while the pitiful howling echoed louder around him. He was getting closer.

Michael Morpurgo

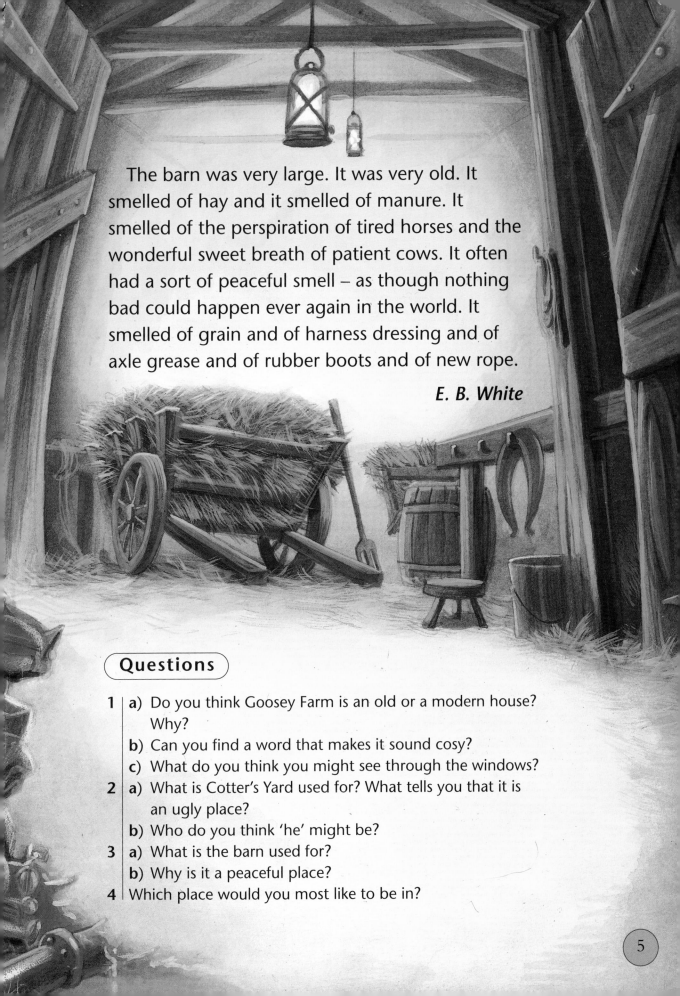

The barn was very large. It was very old. It smelled of hay and it smelled of manure. It smelled of the perspiration of tired horses and the wonderful sweet breath of patient cows. It often had a sort of peaceful smell – as though nothing bad could happen ever again in the world. It smelled of grain and of harness dressing and of axle grease and of rubber boots and of new rope.

E. B. White

Questions

1 a) Do you think Goosey Farm is an old or a modern house? Why?
   b) Can you find a word that makes it sound cosy?
   c) What do you think you might see through the windows?
2 a) What is Cotter's Yard used for? What tells you that it is an ugly place?
   b) Who do you think 'he' might be?
3 a) What is the barn used for?
   b) Why is it a peaceful place?
4 Which place would you most like to be in?

All about Spiders

'First,' said Charlotte, 'I dive at him.' She plunged headfirst towards the fly. As she dropped, a tiny silken thread unwound from her rear end.

'Next, I wrap him up.' She grabbed the fly, threw a few jets of silk round it, and rolled it over and over, wrapping it so that it couldn't move. Wilbur watched in horror. He could hardly believe what he was seeing, and although he detested flies he was sorry for this one.

10 'There!' said Charlotte. 'Now I knock him out, so he'll be more comfortable.' She bit the fly. 'He can't feel a thing now,' she remarked. 'He'll make a perfect breakfast for me.'

'You mean you *eat* flies?' gasped Wilbur.

E. B. White

Spiders

Spiders live in many different places. Some live in our own homes and gardens. Others live on mountains or in deserts. Most of the 60,000 different kinds of spiders are very useful to us. They eat lots of flies and other pests. All spiders have eight legs and can spin silk.

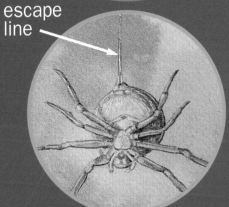

Silk is made by special organs in the abdomen.

silk

escape line

This spider spins a silk thread as an escape line.

This spider wraps its prey in silken threads.

cocoon

Spiders spin a silk cocoon to protect their eggs.

Questions

1. How do you know which piece is fiction?
2. The second piece is from an information book. How can you tell?
3. How do the pictures help you to guess what *abdomen* and *cocoon* mean?
4. Read the captions (the words under the pictures). What things were mentioned in the first piece as well?
5. a) What *more* does the second piece tell you about spiders' silk?
   b) Can you guess what else the spider spins thread for?

Nature's Numbers

One old observant owl
Two tame tickled trout
Three thirsty throated thrushes
Four fine fantailed fish
Five fantastically famous frogs
Six swiftly swimming salmon
Seven sweetly singing songbirds
Eight engagingly eager eels
Nine nippy and neighbourly newts
Ten tenderly tiptoeing tortoises.

John Cotton

Questions

1. Which sounds are repeated in the sixth line?
2. Can you think of any other words that begin with 'sw' that could have been used in the poem?
3. In the first line which word is unusual?
   Find two other words you like and say why.
4. Does anyone know any other tongue twisters?

Rita the Rescuer

Nearby in Jubilee Gardens a large crowd had gathered beneath a tree.

'That cat's going to fall!' someone yelled.

'Our poor little Rufus!' cried Mr and Mrs Rumbold.

'Hang on, Rufus!' called Rita. 'Here I come!'
She whooshed through the air like a whirlwind.

'Ooh!' gasped the crowd.

'Got you!' said Rita and she snatched Rufus to safety just as his claws slipped from the branch.

10 'Thank you! Thank you!' cried Mr and Mrs Rumbold, but Rita was off again – she had heard another call for help.

Eddie's go-cart was out of control and hurtling down the steepest hill in town.

Rita ran like a greyhound. She grabbed the go-cart and braked so hard with her heels that sparks flew in the air.

'Phew!' said Eddie, as they screeched to a halt. 'That was a very close thing!'

20 At the foot of the hill a crowd stood and stared.

Mr Carter's mare, Rosie, had fallen down a hole in the road. No one knew how to get her out.

But help was at hand.

Speeding down the street came
– a jet plane?
– a javelin?
– a flash of greased lightning?

No! It was Rita the Rescuer.

Rita dived down the hole.

30 'One – two – three – heave!' she cried.

She raised Rosie above her head.

'Up you go!' she said and she lifted Rosie out of
the hole and placed her back safely on the road.

'What strength!' cried the crowd.

'What muscles! Did you ever see anything like it?'

They cheered and they clapped and Rosie swished
her tail.

'Goodbye, everybody!' said Rita. 'I'm off home for
my tea!'

Hilda Offen

Questions

1 a) Why is Rita called Rita the Rescuer?
   b) Who does she rescue?
2 a) How would you read aloud the lines, 'That cat's going
      to fall!'?
   b) What tells you how they should be read?
3 Can you find any words which tell you how to read what
   the characters say?
4 How would you read lines 24–7? What are the dashes for?

Catalogue Cats

'Would you boys like to plant gardens?' my father said.

'Yes,' we said.

'Good!' said my father. 'I'll order a catalogue.'

So it was settled. But afterwards, Huey said to me, 'What's a catalogue?'

'A catalogue,' I said, 'is where cats come from. It's a big book full of
10 pictures of hundreds and hundreds of cats. And when you open it up, all the cats jump out and start running around.'

'I don't believe you,' Huey said.

'It's true,' I said.

'But why would Dad be sending for that catalogue cat book?'

'The cats help with the garden,' I said.

20 'I don't believe you,' Huey said.

'It's true,' I said. 'You open the catalogue, and the cats jump out. Then they run outside and work in the garden. White cats dig up the ground with their claws. Black cats brush the ground smooth with their tails. Yellow and brown cats roll on the

seeds to push them underground so they
can grow.'

30   'I don't believe you,' Huey said. 'Cats
don't act like that.'

'Of course,' I said, '*ordinary* cats
don't act like that. That's why you
have to get them specially –
catalogue cats.'

'Really?' Huey said.

'Really,' I said.

'I'm going to ask Dad about it,'
Huey said.

40   'You ask Dad about everything,' I said.
'Don't you think it's time you learned
something on your own for a change?'
Huey looked hurt. 'I do learn things by myself,'
he said. 'I wonder when the catalogue will come.'

'Soon,' I said.

The next morning Huey woke me up. 'I dreamed
about the catalogue cats!' he said.

Anne Cameron

(**Questions**)

1 | What do you think the catalogue really has in it?
2 | Why does his brother tell Huey that a catalogue
is where cats come from?
3 | Why does Huey want to ask his dad about it?
4 | Who is speaking in lines 16–17?
5 | How does the punctuation help you to know
how the characters say their words?

13

SEED CATALOGUE

A packet of seed can be a cheap way to get a lot of flowers BUT … don't go seed-mad. Growing plants from seed is slow. It can be a tricky, fiddly business, and not all seeds will grow just by being tipped in the ground.

   If you like the picture on a packet of seed, read the print on the back! The seeds may need starting off in a box of special compost, in a glass frame, or in a heated greenhouse.

Flowers which can be grown from seed

These are all annual plants: their life cycle is over in one year. They are all sown out of doors in the open ground in spring. Some bloom longer than others, but all give a good flowering, most of them from June to September. They are all easy to grow. They *all* like a sunny place.

10

20

30

SUTTONS SEEDS

BY APPOINTMENT TO HER MAJESTY THE QUEEN SEEDSMEN SUTTONS SEEDS LIMITED

BY APPOINTMENT TO HER MAJESTY QUEEN ELIZABETH THE QUEEN MOTHER SEEDSMEN, SUTTONS SEEDS LIMITED

NASTURTIUM
JEWEL MIXED

NASTURTIUM
JEWEL MIXED
Hardy Annual
(Sow direct outside)

12 39 €

Height Appro
23–30cm (9–12 in.

SOW

PLANTING OUT

FLOWERIN
HARVEST

JAN	FEB	MAR	APR	MAY	JUN	JUL	AUG	SEP	OCT	NOV	DEC

DESCRIPTION. Brightly coloured large flowers held well above succulent mid-green compact foliage. Flowers in shades of orange, red and yellow.

SOWING/GROWING. Sow the seed thinly direct into finely raked, moist warm, weed free soil where the plants are to flower 13mm. (½in.) deep. As the seedlings develop, thin to achieve a final spacing of 25cm. (10ins.). Alternatively, for hanging baskets and containers sow on a window sill or in a greenhouse at approx. 13–18°C (55–65°F) 3 or 4 seeds to a 7.5cm. (3ins.) pot. Plant after acclimatisation to outside conditions.

HELPFUL HINT. For very best results grow Jewel Mixed on poor soil, in a bright sunny position.

QUALITY CONTROL
The seed in thi

Alyssum	White, pink, purple; 7 cm tall. Sow in May.	85p *per packet*
Bartonia	Yellow; 45 cm high. Sow in April.	90p
Calendula	(Marigolds.) Orange; 30 to 45 cm tall. Very easy. Sow in April and May.	95p
Candytuft	White, mauve, crimson; 20 to 30 cm tall. Sow in April.	85p
Cornflower	White, pink, blue; 30 cm tall. Dwarf kinds are best. Sow in April and May.	90p
Linaria	Like midget snapdragons. Mixed colours; 20 to 30 cm tall. Sow in April and May.	95p
Nasturtium	Red, orange, yellow; 22 to 30 cm high. Sow in May.	95p

Questions

1 a) What does the word *catalogue* mean?
   b) Look up the word *catalogue* in a dictionary.
2 a) What does this extract from the catalogue describe?
   b) What other kinds of seeds can you think of?
3 a) What kinds of flowers are in this list?
   b) Do you think they would be suitable for the two boys in Unit 5? (see page 12)
4 a) Look at the seed packet. How does it tell you when to sow the seeds?
   b) Can you find these flowers in the seed catalogue?

A Poem to be Spoken Silently

It was so quiet that I heard
a fly rub its greedy hands.

It was so quiet that I heard
a blade of grass break through
the Spring earth.

It was so quiet that I heard
my pencil scratch across
the empty sheet.

It was so quiet that I heard
10 my tired eyelids flicker.

It was so quiet that I heard
the moment between the tick
and the tock
of the classroom clock.

It was so quiet that I heard
the next line of this poem
slip into my buzzing mind
and spill
onto the silent page.

Pie Corbett

Questions

1 | Which do you think is the quietest sound?
2 | There is one adjective in verse one, and one in verse three.
Are they well chosen? Can you think of better ones?
3 | Look at the verbs in the first two verses. Two are strong ones.
Try replacing them with different verbs. What is the effect?
4 | If you had amazingly good hearing, what sound do you
think your eyelids closing might make?

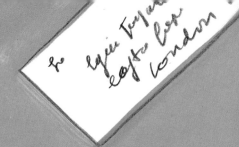

Flat Stanley

A board falls on Stanley when he's asleep. In the morning he's as flat as a pancake. But although he's only a centimetre thick, he feels fine. Soon he begins to enjoy all the things he can do. His brother Arthur gets quite jealous. [* means sound effects go here.]

Mr Lambchop Come in at once. There's a letter here from the Jeffrey family.*

Mrs Lambchop The Jeffrey family have gone to live in California. What do they say?

Mr Lambchop They have invited Stanley to visit them for his holidays.

Stanley Oh boy! I would love to go!

Mrs Lambchop It would be a wonderful trip for him, George. But an aeroplane ticket to California is
10 very expensive.

Mr Lambchop Well, what about this for size?

Arthur What is it?

Mrs Lambchop It looks like an enormous, brown-paper envelope.

Mr Lambchop It *is* an enormous brown-paper envelope. I made it while you were out. Don't you see? We can send Stanley by post, just for the price of the stamps.

Mrs Lambchop It doesn't sound right at all. I've never heard of sending boys by post for their holidays.

20 **Mr Lambchop** Not everyone has a flat boy to send.

Arthur Can I be the one to drop him in the post box? I want to hear him go PLOP!

Mrs Lambchop That will do, Arthur. We'll try it, but I can't say I really like the idea of sending a son of mine through the post.

Stanley But what about food? How will I get anything to eat if I'm stuck down in an envelope?

Mr Lambchop Let's try you for size first, Stanley. Just slide in and then we can see if there's any room left over for a sandwich.

Stanley Hooray! Look, there's plenty of room. Have you got an egg one?

Mrs Lambchop Get your flat cigarette case, George, and I'll fill it with milk.

Mr Lambchop There you are Stanley. You've got an egg salad sandwich and a cigarette case full of milk. What more could a boy want? I'll just stick a few extra stamps on the envelope.

Arthur I'll put them on. I'll bang them down well, too. ★

Stanley Owwwww! That was *me* you were banging, Arthur Lambchop.

Mrs Lambchop Shame on you, Arthur. Your father will do the rest. We shall have to put a great many stamps on, because there's the insurance as well as the ordinary air mail. I can't post a son of mine without having him insured.

Mr Lambchop But it's still much less expensive than a train or an aeroplane ticket would be.

Arthur Can I be the one to drop him in the letter box? He'll make a fine PLOP!

Mrs Lambchop Your father will do the posting, Arthur. Come along, George. I can't help feeling nervous.

I really don't know whether it's right to send a boy through the post. After all, Stanley has never been away from home alone before.

Mr Lambchop Not everyone has a flat boy to send. Come along. We'll go to the letter box on the corner.

Mrs Lambchop I seem to remember that letter box has rather a small slit. It isn't nearly big enough for posting a
60   boy.

Mr Lambchop Okay! Okay! I'll just fold the envelope over like this and then Stanley can get himself straight again when he's inside. Ready, my boy? Down you go then!★

Stanley WHOOPS!

Mrs Lambchop Can you hear me down there, dear? Are you all right?

Stanley Okay. I'm fine. Can I eat my sandwich now?

Mr Lambchop What did I tell you? He's all right. Boys who want to eat sandwiches are always all right.

70   **Mrs Lambchop** Wait an hour, then you can eat it. And try not to get overheated, dear. Goodbye!

Mr Lambchop Goodbye!

Stanley Goodbyeeee!

Jeff Brown (adapted by Sheila Lane and Marion Kemp)

(**Questions**)

1 | What sounds would you make at each ★?
2 | How can you tell that Arthur is jealous?
3 | Find some lines where Mrs Lambchop is fussing. How would you read them?
4 | How does Mr Lambchop feel about posting Stanley? Find the lines that make you think this.
5 | How would you like to be sent through the post like a letter? What are some of the things that might happen?

Word Pictures

A Flamingo

A Flamingo
is
a
long
cooooooooooooool
drink
of
something pink

J Patrick Lewis

In this box

In this box I keep my secret
things like foreign coins wi
th holes in them, a ru
bber in the shape of a
n elephant, a thimble whic
h is made of china and a
brass button that has an
eagle on it. There are ot
her things I keep to myself

Here is the key to fit my box

John Fairfax

Questions

1. Why has the poet written cooooooooool instead of 'cool'?
2. Name two things found in the box.
3. What is special about the rubber and the button?
4. Which poem do you like better and why?
5. Suggest some other objects or creatures that might make a good shape poem.

Map Reading

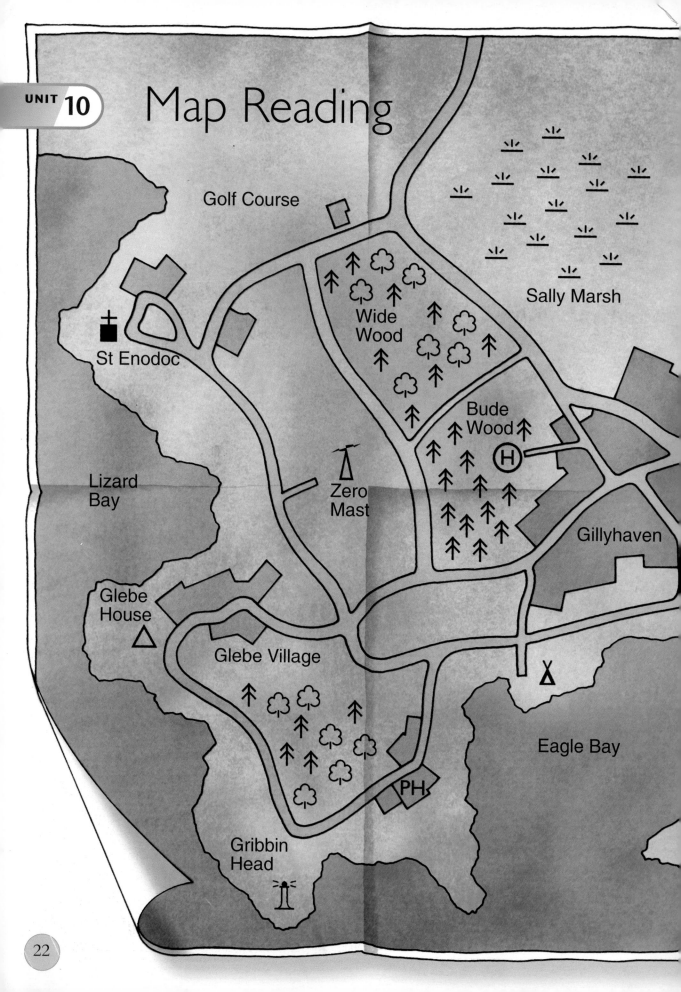

Golf Course

Sally Marsh

St Enodoc

Wide Wood

Bude Wood

H

Lizard Bay

Zero Mast

Gillyhaven

Glebe House

Glebe Village

Eagle Bay

PH

Gribbin Head

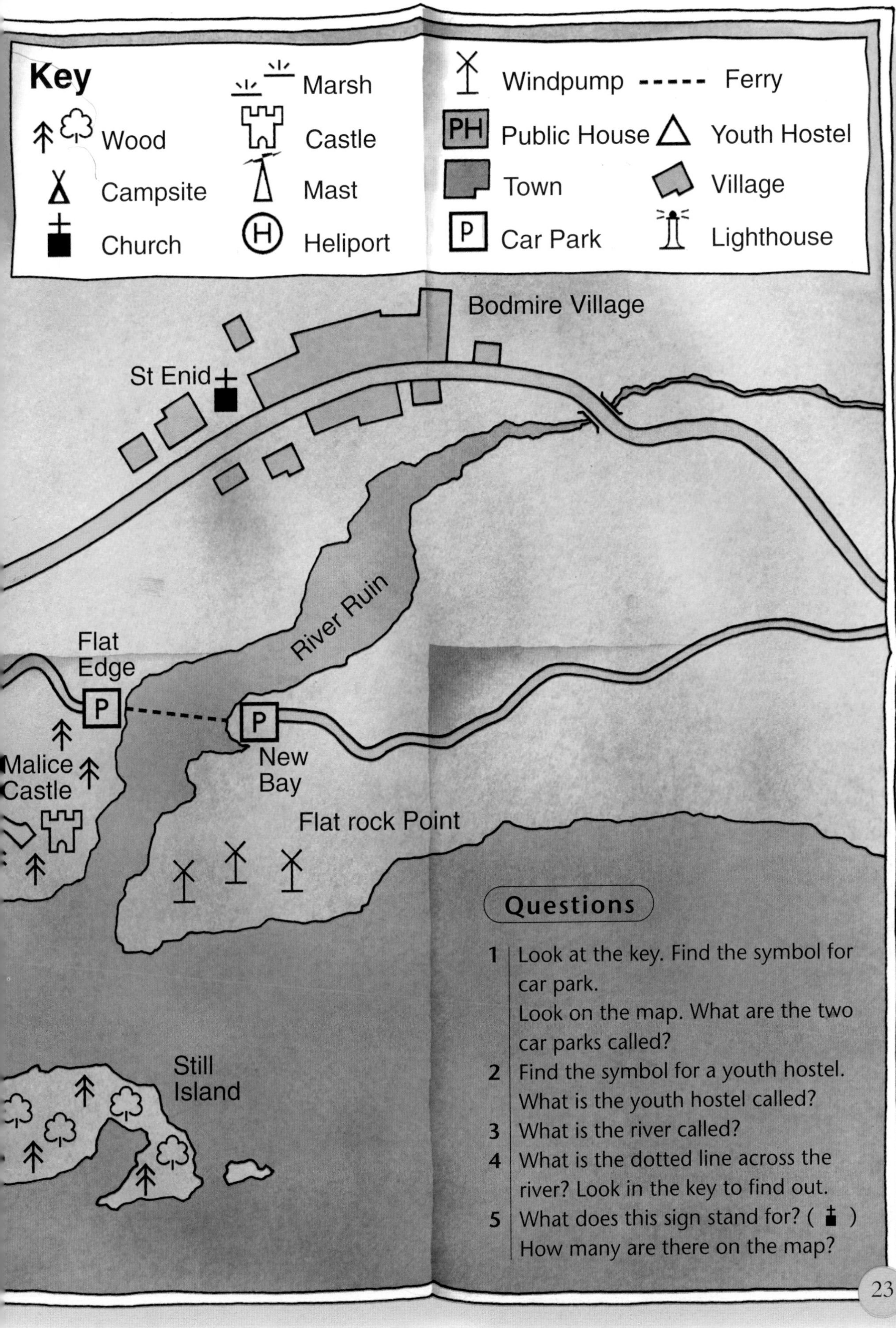

Key

- 🌳 Wood
- ⛺ Campsite
- ⛪ Church
- 🔆 Marsh
- 🏰 Castle
- 🗼 Mast
- Ⓗ Heliport
- 🎐 Windpump
- PH Public House
- ⬛ Town
- P Car Park
- - - - - - Ferry
- △ Youth Hostel
- ◇ Village
- 🗼 Lighthouse

Bodmire Village

St Enid ✝

River Ruin

Flat Edge

P

Malice Castle 🏰

P

New Bay

Flat rock Point

🎐 🎐 🎐

Still Island

Questions

1 Look at the key. Find the symbol for car park.
Look on the map. What are the two car parks called?

2 Find the symbol for a youth hostel. What is the youth hostel called?

3 What is the river called?

4 What is the dotted line across the river? Look in the key to find out.

5 What does this sign stand for? (✝) How many are there on the map?

23

The Five Keys

Look at the map on pages 22–3.

These instructions will help you travel from Still Island to the church of St Enodoc. On your journey you will find five keys.

For your journey, you will need the following:

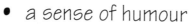

- a brave heart
- swift feet and strong arms
- a white pebble
- a voice to shout with
- a sense of humour

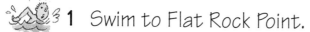

You will find a white pebble on the beach. Now you are ready, here is what you must do.

 1 Swim to Flat Rock Point.

2 By the third windpump you will find the first key.

 **3** Walk to New Bay and catch the ferry to Flat Edge.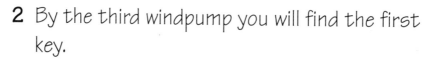

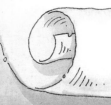 **4** Run to the castle as there are wolves nearby.

5 At the castle, shout into the well. When you hear your echo, throw in the pebble for good luck.

 6 Walk to Gribbin Head. At the top of the lighthouse is the second key.

 7 Walk back up the road and through Bude Wood to the heliport. You will be given the third key by another traveller.

 **8** Run through Wide Wood to the golf course. The fourth key is hidden in one of the holes!

 9 Take the road towards St Enodoc. The fifth key is in the church tower.

 10 Walk round Lizard Bay to Glebe Village. Leave the five keys at the youth hostel. Your journey is at an end.

Pie Corbett

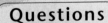

Questions

1 | What do you learn in the first paragraph?
2 | What are the bullet points used for?
3 | How many instructions are there?
4 | Where does the journey begin?
5 | Where does the journey end?
6 | Where is the second key?

One Fine Morning

One fine morning, a kind and good-natured peasant, named Jan, decided to go into the world to seek his fortune. His father gave him his blessing and two silver sixpences, and away he went into the woods whistling a merry tune.

Chris Buckton

Once upon a time, in a grand palace, there lived a lord who had a daughter named Gretchen, who was as clever as she was good, and pretty besides. Rich merchants and noblemen came from all over the country to ask her hand in marriage, but her father would have none of them. 'The man who marries my daughter,' said he, 'must be the best huntsman in the world.'

Now in the village nearby there was a poor widow's
10 son called Hans, who got it into his head that he would like to marry Gretchen himself. 'Alas, poor boy, that can never be,' said his mother; for though Hans was a good-natured lad and she loved him dearly, yet he was a bit simple.

Alison Lurie

There was once a baker who lived in a little village. He had two daughters. Though they were twins, yet they were as different as summer and winter. One was generous and good-natured, while the other was selfish, greedy and cross.

Alison Lurie

Questions

1. Look at the first few words of these story openings. What do you notice about them?
2. The same kinds of people often turn up in traditional tales. Can you spot some of them here?
3. Where do these stories take place?
4. Can you guess what the last few words of these stories might be?

Finders Keepers

Ten things found in the shipwrecked sailor's pocket

A litre of sea.

An unhappy jellyfish.

A small piece of a lifeboat.

A pencil wrapped around with seaweed.

A soaking feather.

The first page of a book called 'Swimming is Easy'.

A folded chart showing dangerous rocks.

A photograph of a little girl in a red dress.

A gold coin.

A letter from a mermaid.

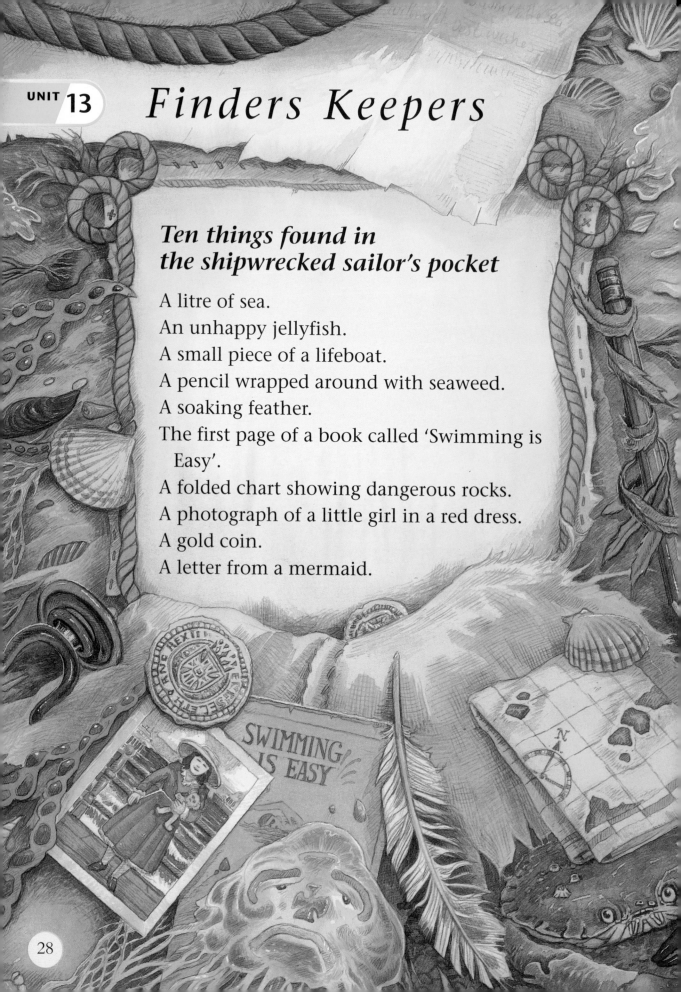

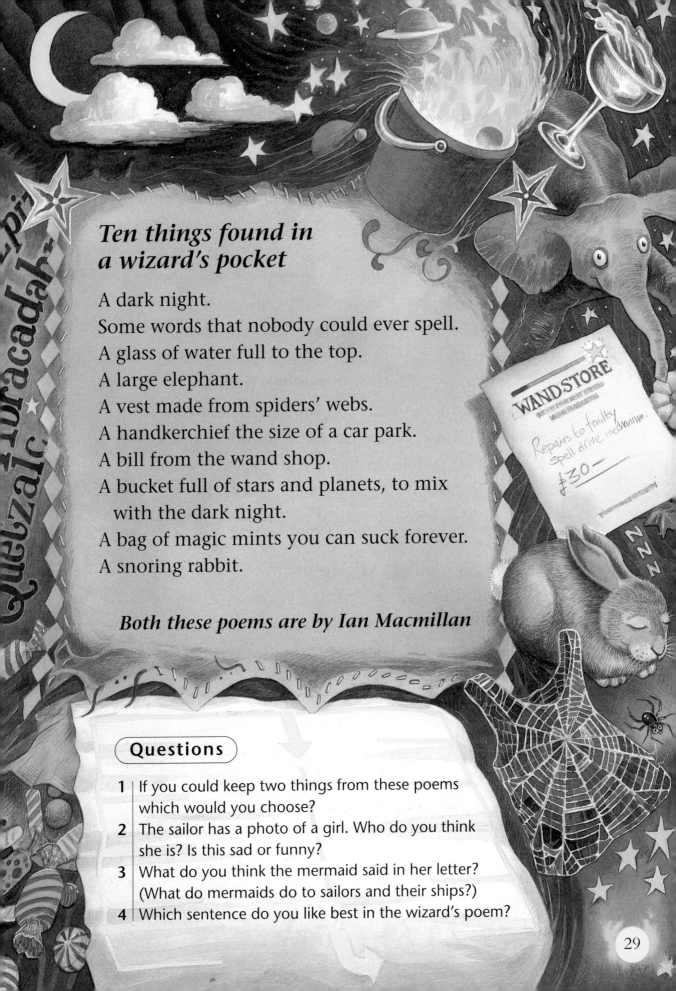

Ten things found in a wizard's pocket

A dark night.
Some words that nobody could ever spell.
A glass of water full to the top.
A large elephant.
A vest made from spiders' webs.
A handkerchief the size of a car park.
A bill from the wand shop.
A bucket full of stars and planets, to mix
  with the dark night.
A bag of magic mints you can suck forever.
A snoring rabbit.

Both these poems are by Ian Macmillan

WANDSTORE

Repairs to faulty
Spell drive mechanism:
£30—

Questions

1 | If you could keep two things from these poems which would you choose?
2 | The sailor has a photo of a girl. Who do you think she is? Is this sad or funny?
3 | What do you think the mermaid said in her letter? (What do mermaids do to sailors and their ships?)
4 | Which sentence do you like best in the wizard's poem?

Skunny-Wundy's Skipping Stone I

Long ago, in a little village by the Otsiningo River, there lived a boy named Skunny-Wundy. He was not as big or as strong as the other boys, but he could do two things better than the others – think fast and skip stones. Though the other boys tried, none beat him at stone skipping. Sometimes they'd ask Skunny-Wundy to join them throwing stones at frogs and turtles on the river bank. Skunny-Wundy would never do that. His mother had told him

10 stories about the animals and he didn't want to hurt them. Almost any day he could be found by the river, skipping stones. Skunny-Wundy always went to the south because of what his parents told him.

'Why must I never go north?' Skunny-Wundy asked.

'Listen,' his mother said. 'To the north there are terrible beings, giants whose skins are made of stone. Arrows and spears bounce off them. They are taller than pine trees! And

20 do you know what they like to eat?'

'People!' said Skunny-Wundy's father.

For a long time, or so it seemed to Skunny-Wundy, he did as his parents said. Whenever he skipped stones on the river he went south. When he returned he never went past his own village. But it grew harder and harder to find good skipping stones.

One day Skunny-Wundy rose very early,

before the sun. No one else was awake. He said to
himself, 'It won't matter if I walk just a *little* way
towards the north. I won't go far.'

As soon as he started north he found a good
skipping stone. Another one, though, further on,
was better! Gradually, he went around the bend in
the river, leaving the village far behind. Finally, as
the sun reached the middle of the sky, he found a
stone that was perfect. It was just the right weight,
smooth and flat. Setting his feet, he cocked his arm
and threw. It skipped twelve times before it sank,
leaving a row of rings on the river's smooth surface.

'WEH-YOH!' Skunny-Wundy shouted. 'I am the
best skipper of stones in the world!'

'HAH-A-AH,' roared a great voice over his head, so
loud it shook the ground under his feet. 'You are not
the greatest skipper of stones!'

Skunny-Wundy looked up. There, looming over
the trees, was the biggest, hungriest-looking stone
giant anyone could imagine. It reached down,
picked up a flat stone as big as a bear and threw it
across the river. That stone skipped fifteen times
before it sank!

'HAH-A-AH,' the stone giant roared again. 'You
see who is the greatest skipper of stones. Now I am
going to eat you.'

Skunny-Wundy knew it would be no good to run.
The stone giant would catch him in one stride. But
he could use his wits.

'Hunh!' Skunny-Wundy said. 'Are you afraid I will
beat you?'

60   'ENHH?' said the stone giant. 'I am afraid of no
one.' He stomped his foot on the ground so hard
it almost knocked Skunny-Wundy off his feet.

    'If you are not afraid,' Skunny-Wundy said, 'we will
have a contest to see who's better at skipping stones.'

    'Nyoh!' the stone giant said. 'I agree. Go ahead.
Throw your stone. Try to beat me.'

    'Ah,' Skunny-Wundy said, 'my arm is too tired
now. I've been skipping stones all day. Let me go
home and rest. I promise I'll come back
70 tomorrow for our contest.'

    Skunny-Wundy ran as fast he could. He didn't
stop until he was within sight of his village. He
sat down on a log and began to laugh. It had
been so easy to outwit the stone giant. Stone
giants were stupid. Then Skunny-Wundy
remembered. He'd given his word he would
return the next day! His parents had always told
him breaking a promise was a terrible thing.
80 Not only that, if he didn't keep his word, the
stone giant might come looking for him. It
only had to follow the river. It wouldn't just
find Skunny-Wundy, but his whole village. It
wouldn't just eat him, it would eat every one.

    When Skunny-Wundy went to bed that
night he was very quiet. His mother asked if
anything was wrong, but Skunny-Wundy said
nothing. If he told his parents, they'd try to
fight the monster. It would eat them too. The
90 next morning, before sunrise, Skunny-Wundy
walked slowly towards the north along the

river, certain that this would be his last day. As he walked, though, he kept looking down. Perhaps if he found just the right stone he'd be able to beat the stone giant. He kept picking up stones and dropping them. None were just right. Then he heard a voice from the ground ahead of him. It was calling his name!

'Skunny-Wundy, Skunny-Wundy. Take me,
100 Skunny-Wundy. Take me, take me, take me.'

Skunny-Wundy looked down among the flat stones. Was one of them talking to him? Then he saw that what he thought to be a stone was a little turtle, its head sticking out of its shell.

'Skunny-Wundy,' the turtle said again, 'take me, take me, take me, take me.'

'You want me to use you as a skipping stone?'

'Nyoh, nyoh, nyoh, nyoh!' said the little turtle. 'We can win, we can win, we can win, we can win!'

110 'All right,' Skunny-Wundy said. 'A small friend is better than no friend at all when you're in trouble.' The little turtle pulled in its head and legs. It looked just like a skipping stone. Then Skunny-Wundy placed the turtle in his belt pouch and continued on.

Joseph Bruchac

(**Questions**)

1 | Skunny-Wundy isn't big and strong, but he does have two skills. What are they?
2 | a) Why do his parents tell him never to go north?
   | b) Why does he disobey them?
3 | How does Skunny-Wundy use his wits when he meets the giant?
4 | Why does Skunny-Wundy take the turtle with him?

Skunny-Wundy's Skipping Stone 2

'KEWH!' rumbled the stone giant as it saw him. 'Little food, I have been waiting for you. Are you ready to be eaten?'

Skunny-Wundy held up his hand. 'Wait!' he said. 'First we must have our contest. Remember?'

'HAH-A-AH!' the stone giant laughed. 'Throw your stone. Then I shall beat you and then I shall eat you.'

10 'No,' Skunny-Wundy said, 'you must go first. You challenged me.'

'NYOH,' the stone giant said. 'That is good.' It picked up a stone as large as a lodge and then, 'HHRRUMMM,' hurled it. It struck the water with a great WHAP! each time it skipped. It skipped seventeen times and knocked down a dozen trees on the other side.

'Now, little food,' the stone giant said, reaching for Skunny-Wundy.

20 'First I must throw my stone,' Skunny-Wundy said, his voice was calm, but his heart was beating so fast he thought it would burst. He reached into his pouch for a stone and found the little turtle. He pulled it out, drew back his arm, and threw! The turtle struck the water just right and started to skip.

One, two, three, four, five, six, seven times it skipped. Eight, nine, ten, eleven, twelve times. But it was slowing down. Just then, the little turtle stuck out its legs and began kicking. Thirteen, fourteen, fifteen times it skipped. Sixteen, seventeen,

30 eighteen, nineteen, twenty times and now it was skipping in circles. Twenty-one, twenty-two, twenty-three, twenty-four times it skipped and then sank beneath the surface.

'WEH-YOH!' Skunny-Wundy shouted. 'I have won. Eat me if you want, but you have lost!'

The stone giant became very angry. It had never been defeated at anything before. It started to shake with rage. It shook and shook. It shook so hard cracks appeared in its body. Flakes of rock flecked

40 from its cheeks. Harder and harder it shook until it collapsed into a pile of little stones.

So it was that with the help of this friend, the little turtle, Skunny-Wundy defeated his first stone giant.

Joseph Bruchac

Questions

1 | Why does Skunny-Wundy ask the giant to throw his stone first?
2 | Why does the giant call Skunny-Wundy 'little food'?
3 | Why does the giant get so angry at the end of the story? What happens to him?
4 | Can you think of any other stories where the weaker characters win by clever tricks?

Big Billy

There's a spider in the bathroom
With legs as thick as rope.
It lives behind the cupboard
Where my mother keeps the soap.
My sister calls it Billy,
She says he creeps each night
Into children's bedrooms
(when they turn out the light).

I lie and hear him coming.
10 I hear his spider breath,
Huffing up the passage
With gasps as dark as death.
I hide beneath my duvet
…but the sides they won't tuck in…
And I know he'll find a pathway
And I know that Billy'll win!

I know he's going to get me.
I know he's going to come
And he's going to eat my sister
20 And he's going to get my mum…
He's going to eat the family,
He's going to eat us all
'Cos Billy's really awful…

…and he's coming up the hall!!!

Peter Dixon

Questions

1 | What sort of person do you think is speaking in the poem?
2 | Who is Big Billy?
3 | What sounds does Billy make as he comes up the passage at night?
4 | In the first verse, who is trying to frighten the speaker?

The Paper Bag Princess

Elizabeth was a beautiful princess. She lived in a castle and had expensive princess clothes.

She was going to marry a prince named Ronald.

Unfortunately, a dragon smashed her castle, burned all her clothes with his fiery breath, and carried off Prince Ronald.

Elizabeth decided to chase the dragon and get Ronald back.

She looked everywhere for something to wear, but
10 the only thing she could find that was not burnt was a paper bag. So she put on the paper bag and followed the dragon.

He was easy to follow because he left a trail of burnt forests and horses' bones.

Finally, Elizabeth came to a cave with a large door that had a huge knocker on it.

She took hold of the knocker and banged on the door.

The dragon stuck his nose out of the door and said, 'Well, a princess! I love to eat princesses. But I have
20 already eaten a whole castle today – I am a very busy dragon. Come back tomorrow.'

He slammed the door so fast that Elizabeth almost got her nose caught.

Elizabeth grabbed the knocker and banged on the door again.

The dragon stuck his nose out of the door and said, 'Go away. I love to eat princesses but I have

already eaten a whole castle today. I am a very busy
30 dragon. Come back tomorrow.'

'Wait,' shouted Elizabeth. 'Is it true that you are the
smartest and fiercest dragon in the whole world?'

'Yes,' said the dragon.

'Is it true,' said Elizabeth, 'that you can burn up ten
forests with your fiery breath?'

'Oh, yes,' said the dragon, and he took a huge, deep
breath and breathed out so much fire that he burnt up
fifty forests.

'Fantastic,' said Elizabeth, and the dragon took
40 another huge breath and breathed out so much fire
that he burnt up one hundred forests.

'Magnificent,' said Elizabeth, and the dragon took
another huge breath, but this time nothing came out.

The dragon didn't even have enough fire left to cook
a meat ball.

Elizabeth said, 'Dragon, is it true that you can fly
around the world in just ten seconds?'

'Why, yes,' said the dragon and jumped up and flew
all the way around the world in just ten seconds.

50   He was very tired when he got back, but Elizabeth shouted, 'Fantastic, do it again!'

So the dragon jumped up and flew around the whole world in just twenty seconds.

When he got back he was too tired to talk and he lay down and went straight to sleep.

Elizabeth whispered very softly, 'Hey, dragon.' The dragon didn't move at all.

She lifted up the dragon's ear and put her head right inside. She shouted as loud as she could, 'Hey, dragon!'

60   The dragon was so tired he didn't even move.

Elizabeth walked right over the dragon and opened the door to the cave.

There was Prince Ronald.

He looked at her and said, 'Elizabeth, you are a mess! You smell like ashes, your hair is all tangled and you are wearing a dirty old paper bag. Come back when you are dressed like a real princess.'

'Ronald,' said Elizabeth, 'your clothes are really pretty and your hair is very neat. You look
70 like a real prince, but you are a toad.'

They didn't get married after all.

Questions

1 | a) How is the princess like other princesses in fairy tales?
    b) How is she different?
2 | Who else in this story would you expect to meet in a fairy tale?
3 | How does Elizabeth trick the dragon?
4 | How would you expect the story to end? How is it different?

YOU!

You!
Your head is like a hollow drum.
You!
Your eyes are like balls of flame.
You!
Your ears are like fans for blowing fire.
You!
Your nostril is like a mouse's hole.
You!
Your mouth is like a lump of mud.
You!
Your hands are like drum-sticks.
You!
Your belly is like a pot of bad water.
You!
Your legs are like wooden posts.
You!
Your backside is like a mountain-top.

From the Igbo people, Africa

Questions

1 | There are exclamation marks after the word 'You'.
How do you think it should be read aloud?
2 | Who do you think the poet is talking to in the poem?
3 | Does the poet like or dislike the person? How do you know?
4 | Find clues that shows the poem comes from another country.
5 | Which is the funniest line?

41

Make a Toy Theatre

You will need an old shoe box, a pencil, a ruler, scissors or a trimming knife, paints, paintbrushes, scraps of metallic paper, and glue.

1 Draw a rectangle 9cm wide and 6cm high on the bottom of the shoe box.

Leave at least 3cm space between the rectangle and the top of the box. Place the rectangle so that there is equal space on either side.

This rectangle will be the stage opening or proscenium.

2 Cut along the sides and bottom of the rectangle. Do not cut along the top edge.

3 Bend the top edge back to form a curtain for the stage.

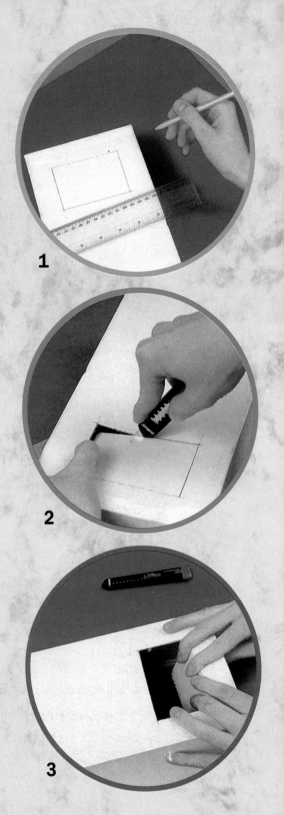

1

2

3

4

4 Paint the box and decorate it with shapes cut from the scraps of metallic paper.

5 Your theatre is now ready. All it needs are puppets. Use finger puppets, or try some paper cone figures *(see pages 25–27).*

5

Questions

1 **a)** Where does it tell you what you will need?
  b) Why does it tell you at the beginning?
  c) How many things on the list do you think are in school already?

2 **a)** What do the numbers mean beside each picture?
  b) Explain each stage in one sentence.

3 Do you think you would know what to do:
  a) if the pictures were not there?
  b) if the words were not there?

4 **a)** What do you think a paper cone figure would look like?
  b) Where would you find out if you had the book?

The Boy Who Went Looking for a Friend

Once there was a little boy called Sam. He said to his mother, 'I am lonely. Where can I find a friend?'

His mother said, 'Behind our house is a field. It is filled with grass and red poppies and cornflowers. There are ears of wild wheat. There are big brown and yellow butterflies. Go into the field, Sam. Perhaps you will find a friend there.'

The little boy went into the field. Among the poppies and the grass he met a tiger. The tiger was as
10 yellow as sunshine. Over his coat were beautiful dark stripes. He had a very long twitching tail. 'Hello, Tiger,' said Sam.

'Hello, Sam,' said the tiger. He yawned a tiger yawn. His teeth looked very white. 'Are you the sort of tiger that eats boys?' asked Sam.

'No!' said the tiger. 'I only eat sandwiches. I have some sandwiches wrapped in lunch paper. Would you like some?' Sam and the tiger had a picnic on the grass. Then they played hide and seek all over the
20 field. They hid up trees and behind trees, and made long secret tunnels through the grass. They had a lot of fun. But at sunset the tiger said, 'I must be going now.'

'Will you come back?' asked Sam.

'Perhaps I will,' said the tiger. 'Or perhaps I won't,' and off he went waving his tail.

[So Sam was still lonely. The next day he met some monkeys in his garden.]

The monkeys made themselves into a long monkey-ladder
30 and Sam climbed up it into the branches. On a big branch of the tree was a table and seventeen chairs. Sam and the monkeys sat down to eat. They ate pancakes and pineapple, sausages and strawberries. They drank raspberry juice out of long clear glasses. Then they all put on funny hats and laughed and sang. However, just as they were all having a lovely time the sun set. The monkeys started to climb the tree. They climbed much faster than Sam could.

'Where are you going to, monkeys?' he called.

40 'Higher up, higher up,' the monkeys squealed.

'Will you come back tomorrow?' asked Sam.

'Perhaps,' said the monkeys, 'or perhaps not.' Off they went, swinging by their tails.

[The next day Sam met a circus in the road.]

The juggler juggled plates and cups and balls and balloons for Sam. He did not drop one. The elephants danced. A lovely fairy girl rode her white horse. She stood on its back, light as a feather, and did not fall off once. The men on the flying trapeze swung to and fro and tossed and
50 turned in the air. Sam clapped and shouted. Most of all he laughed at Jimmy, the funny clown, riding his donkey

backwards. Then it was sunset. The circus began to go on down the road.

'Where are you going?' called Sam.

'Farther on! Father one!' called Jimmy the funny clown.

'Will you ever come back?' asked Sam.

'Perhaps we will, or perhaps we won't,' said Jimmy. Off they went round a bend in the road.

60 The next day Sam was too sad to ask his mother where he could find a friend.

'All my friends go away,' he thought. 'They all go to places where I can't go.' He went down to the river. He sat with his feet in the watercress. Then round a bend in the river came a little boat with a blue sail. It came past Sam. Then it stopped by the watercress and a boy got out. He was just Sam's size of boy, with an ordinary brown face and brown hair.

'Hello!' he said. 'I didn't know you lived here. My 70 name is Philip. What's your name?'

'Sam!' said Sam.

'Get in my boat and we will sail some more,' said Philip. They sailed all afternoon. Up and down the river bank they went, watching the fish in the clear green water. They saw wild ducks swimming and cows coming down to drink. They saw a wild, bright pheasant in the long grass. All the time they talked and made up stories. It was the best day of all. When

80 it was sunset Philip said, 'We must go home now or our mothers will come calling us. May I come and play with you tomorrow, Sam? You are a good sort of friend to share my boat with me.'

'Of course,' said Sam, very pleased. 'We've had a good time, haven't we?'

'Tomorrow will be even better,' said Philip.

Sam went home and said to his mother, 'I've got a friend, Mother, and it isn't a tiger, and it isn't monkeys, and it isn't a circus. It's a boy called Philip.'

90 'That's good', said his mother. 'Tigers are good friends for tigers. Monkeys are good friends for monkeys, and a circus is everybody's friend, but a boy is the best friend for a boy.'

Margaret Mahy

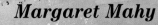

Questions

1 | What is the first animal Sam meets?
Where does he meet it and what do they do together?
2 | Who does he meet next? And what do they do?
3 | Where does he meet the circus and who does he see?
Who does he like best?
4 | Why don't the tiger, monkeys and circus people become Sam's real friends? What is different about Philip?
5 | What do you think Sam will do on the fifth day?

An A to Z of Items Found on the School Roof by the Caretaker

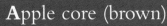

Apple core (brown)
'Better English' book
    (spotted with ink)
Crisps (unopened bag)
Dead bird (a starling
    … I think)

Earwig (inside a matchbox)
Felt pens in a case
    (thirty!)
Golf ball
Handkerchief
    (dirty!)

Ink cartridge (full)
Jaguar
    (model car)

Key (rusty)
Lunch box
    (labelled Paul Starr)

Marble (a bluey)
Nose
    (false one: red)
Orange (all shrivelled)
Pencil (chewed at one end:
    no lead)

Queen's crown (from 2J's play)
Ruler
    (broken: old design)
Sock (shocking pink)
Tennis ball
    (mine)

Underpants (Y-fronts)
Valentine Card
    (to 'Farida Good')
Wellington boot
Xylophone block
    (wood)

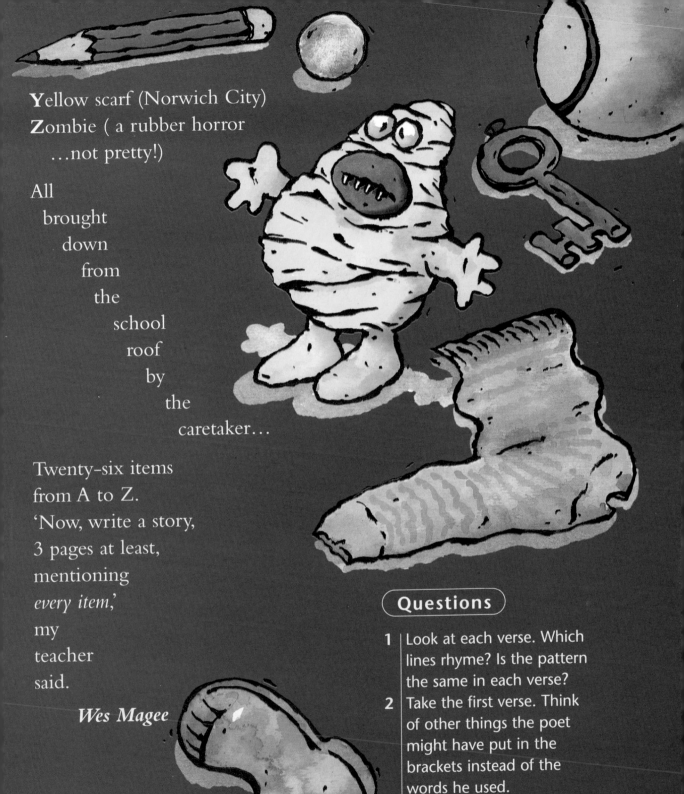

Yellow scarf (Norwich City)
Zombie (a rubber horror
    ...not pretty!)

All
  brought
    down
      from
        the
          school
            roof
              by
                the
                  caretaker...

Twenty-six items
from A to Z.
'Now, write a story,
3 pages at least,
mentioning
every item,'
my
teacher
said.

Wes Magee

Questions

1 Look at each verse. Which lines rhyme? Is the pattern the same in each verse?
2 Take the first verse. Think of other things the poet might have put in the brackets instead of the words he used.
3 Why do you think the poet wrote the second to last verse in a slope?
4 What is the silliest or strangest thing found on the roof?

49

YELLOW PAGES

CATKIN HOME

We cater for –

- Holiday periods
- Sick care
- Long stays
- and your dog as well!

phone now on 23076

CATTERIES

Catkin Home,
  5 Fudge Ave *(see advert)*..23076
Kittycare,
  7 Sunny Road 62312
Prettypaws,
  2 Dale Close...................42817

CAVES

Causley Caves,
  Forest of Doon 42912

CHARITY SHOPS

Age Concern,
  4 Business Park...............44492
Oxfam,
  6 Rosepath Crescent........26803
RSPCA, North Hill 60382

CHILDREN'S ENTERTAINERS

Colin the Clown,
  23 Perrot's Brook.............92176
Mr Jolly, 4 Lower Hill 54321

Give your children's party
the Magic Touch
of

Mr Magic

- juggling
- unicycling
- balloon animals
- jokes
- songs
- rabbits from hats
- puppets
- illusions
- games
- fun for all

phone 33079 – it's not a trick.

Mr Magic,
23 Eastcliff
(see advert).......................33079
Professor Parrot,
5 Penrise.........................27002

CHIMNEY SWEEPS

Brushwork,
12 Eggbuck Road 81045
Bill-the-Brush,
36a Calling Hill 62986
Cleansweep,
Provident Ave
(see advert).....................12498
'Goodasnew',
12 Boddam Close 76502
Vac & Brush,
2 Manadon Crescent........22002

MAKE A CLEAN SWEEP

We will make your chimney clean as a whistle.

• No mess left behind.
• Birds' nests no problem.

Call at Provident Avenue or phone 12498

Questions

1 | How many main headings are there?
2 | What letter of the alphabet does this section follow?
3 | Would you look for this page near the start of the book, in the middle or near the end?
4 | Under which heading are Mr Jolly and Colin the Clown?
5 | What would you ask 'Bill-the-Brush' to do?

Storm

'Come on up, Annie,' said the horseman.

'It's all right,' said Annie, shaking her head.

'I'll take you,' said the horseman.

'You'll be fine,' said Mrs Carter.

'I can walk,' insisted Annie.

But the horseman quickly bent down and put a hand under one of Annie's shoulders and swung her up onto the saddle in front of him as if she were as light as thistledown.

Annie's heart was beating fearfully. She bit hard on her lower lip.

Then the horseman raised one hand and spurred his horse. Mr and Mrs Carter stood and watched as Annie turned away the full white moon of her face and then she and the horseman were swallowed in the stormy darkness.

At first Annie said nothing and the horseman said nothing. But as the horse slowed to a trot and then began to wade across the ford, the horseman asked quietly, 'Are you afraid, Annie?'

'I am,' said Annie. 'I'm afraid for my sister and her baby,' she said. 'And I'm afraid of meeting the ghost.' She paused and then added in a sort of sob, 'I think I'd die if I met him tonight.'

30   At first the horseman didn't reply, and Annie thought it best not to say anything about being rather afraid of him as well, not knowing who he was. But then the rider suddenly reined in. 'Annie,' he said, 'your sister and her baby will be all right.'

'How do you know?' asked Annie.

'And you'll be all right,' said the horseman. 'There are ghosts and ghosts, Annie. Kind ghosts and unkind ghosts. You won't meet the ghost you fear between here and Waterslain.'

40   And so, step by step, Annie and the horseman slowly crossed the ford.

Now the chestnut mare quickened her stride again. It comforted Annie to feel the mare's warm neck and flanks, and after a while she leaned forward and buried her face in its mane.

With her eyes closed, Annie had the sense that she was not so much riding as flying – flying through the storm on a journey that might last forever.

'He's a ghost himself,' thought Annie.

Kevin Crossley-Holland

Questions

1 a) Why is Annie frightened?
   b) What words in the story show how frightened she is?
2 How are Annie and the horseman 'swallowed' in the darkness?
3 Why do you think Annie's parents let her go with the horseman? Does he seem dangerous?
4 What does the horseman mean when he says *'There are ghosts and ghosts'*?
5 *'He's a ghost himself,' thought Annie.* What do you think?

Dear Mr and Mrs Bear

Dear Mr and Mrs Bear
        and Baby Bear,

   I am very sory indeed that I cam into your house and ate Baby Bears porij.  Mummy says I am a bad girl. I hardly eat any porij when she cooks it she sxays. Daddy says he will mend the littel chair.

        Love from
        Goldilocks

P.S. Baby Bear can come to my party if he likes. Ther will be 3 kinds of jelly and a conjoora.

Questions

1 | Why has Goldilocks written this letter?
2 | What has Goldilocks done? Why does her Mum say she's a bad girl?
3 | Does the letter sound really sorry? Will the bears forgive her?
4 | What does P.S. mean?
5 | a) How does Goldilocks begin and end her letter?
  | b) Do you know any other ways of beginning and ending letters?

Insects

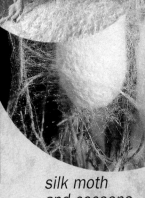
bee

The word insect is often used to describe all sorts of 'creepy-crawlies'. Sometimes, it is difficult to decide whether you have found an insect. There is one good way to tell. Adult insects have six legs.
You might think that a spider is an insect – but spiders have eight legs, so they are not insects.

aphids

Some people do not like insects. They squash them. However, many insects are very helpful to us. For instance, bees make honey and pollinate flowers and trees. Silk moths make silk.

silk moth and cocoons

In the garden, the ladybirds are not only beautiful but also very helpful. They eat aphids. Aphids are insects which kill plants. They look like small green or black flies. (You might have seen them on rose leaves).
    The female ladybird lays her eggs near aphids. When the grubs hatch out they eat the aphids. One ladybird can eat up to 500 aphids. So, make sure that you look after ladybirds. They make great gardeners!

Questions

1   'Garden Creatures'   'An Introduction to Insects'   'Wild Insects'
  Which would make the best title for this extract?
2   What is the important fact in the first paragraph?
3   a) Is a spider an insect?
  b) How do you know?
4   'Squashing Insects'   'Some Insects Are Helpful'   'How To Make Silk'
  Which would you call the third paragraph? Why?
5   Can you name an insect which is *not* helpful?

ladybirds

The Snowgirl

After dinner two more children came to school and started making a snowman together, which was seventeen snowmen in the playground and nearly all of them had carrot noses and biscuit buttons and old black hats. But Tashi's was quite different.

'Whatever's that?' Cheng said.

'A snowman can't have long hair and fruit-gum ear-rings!' Sam said.

'But a snowgirl can,' said Tashi.

10 'Whoever heard of a snowgirl?' said Sam and Cheng. Nobody had.

Then Miss Smith came up the steps with a new yellow toboggan under her arm.

'I'm going to judge the Best Snowman Competition in just a minute,' she said, and then she stopped. 'What's that?'

'It's a snowgirl,' said Tashi and then everybody started talking at once and all the boys were saying, 'How can a snowgirl be in a
20 snowman's competition?' and 'Wouldn't be fair,' and 'Be like having a cat in a dog show,' and things like that.

'Oh dear,' said Miss Smith.

Then Sam said, 'Let's have a hands-up. A hands-up is fair. A hands-up is ever so fair. You can't have fairer than a hands-up, can you?'

'All right,' said Miss Smith. 'We'll have a hands-up.
30 Hands-up all those who think a snowgirl should be
allowed in our competition.' Seven girls' hands shot up.
'Now hands-up all those who think a snowgirl should
not be in the competition. Hands up for *No*.'

All the boys in the playground put their hands up
and that was fourteen.

'That's more than half,' said Miss Smith. '*No* has won.'

'That's not fair,' said Tashi and Tracey and Holly.
'Because there's more boys. It's boys against girls.'

'Oh dear,' said Miss Smith.

40 'A hands-up is ever so fair,' the boys said. 'You can't
change the rules just because you lose. You can't get
fairer than a hands-up.'

Miss Smith walked round all sixteen snowmen and
one snowgirl and you could see she was thinking hard.

'All the snowmen are good and some are very good,'
she said. 'And Tashi's snowgirl is very interesting
indeed, but Sam and Cheng's snowman is excellent and
wins first prize. You'll have to share the yellow
toboggan though, boys.'

Geraldine Kaye

(**Questions**)

1   a) What do most of the snowmen look like?
    b) What is different about Tashi's?
2   Why do you think the boys don't want the snowgirl in
    the competition? Is it just because it's a girl?
3   How do they decide whether the snowgirl should be
    allowed in the competition? Do you think it's fair?
4   What do you imagine Miss Smith was thinking about?
    (lines 43–4)
5   Do you agree with her decision?

Do You Know My Teacher?

She's got a piercing stare
and long black. . .
- (a) moustache
- (b) hair
- (c) teeth
- (d) shoes

She eats chips and beef
and has short sharp. . .
- (a) nails
- (b) fangs
- (c) doorstoppers
- (d) teef

She is slinky and thin
and has a pointed. . .
- (a) banana
- (b) chin
- (c) beard
- (d) umbrella

She has a long straight nose
and hairy little. . .
- (a) kneecaps
- (b) ears
- (c) children
- (d) toes

She has sparkling eyes
and wears school. . .
   (a) dinners
   (b) trousers
   (c) ties
   (d) buses

She comes from down south
and has a very big. . .
   (a) vocabulary
   (b) handbag
   (c) bottom
   (d) mouth

She yells like a preacher,
yes, that's my
   (a) budgie
   (b) stick
   (c) padlock
   (d) teacher!

John Rice

(**Questions**)

1 | What does the teacher like to eat?
2 | Is her nose crooked?
3 | How does the poet describe her eyes?
4 | What might be the funniest choice of words
   for each verse?

59

Allan Ahlberg

Miss Brick the Builder's Baby

So when Baby Brick was born,
Mr and Mrs Brick were very happy.
'Now we have another builder
in the family!' they said.
But did they really have
another builder in the family?
No, they did not.
Mr Brick was a builder.
Mrs Brick was a builder.
Baby Brick was *not* a builder.

This is the house that Baby Brick…

…knocked down!

And this!　　　　　　　And this!

The Vanishment of Thomas Tull

When his tenth birthday arrived Thomas Tull
was so small he had to stand on the *cake* to
blow his candles out.

One of his birthday presents was a toy fort
complete with half a dozen matchstick-firing
cannons and a set of soldiers. Soon Thomas
began living in the fort. His father made a
small bed for him which fitted into it and
Thomas felt comfortable in the company of the
soldiers who were all just that bit smaller than
he was.

From now on Thomas Tull no longer went to
school and his sister Annabelle was told not to
dress him up any more for fear that she might
accidentally squash him. Also the Tulls' cat was
sent away to stay with Thomas's grandma in
another town. But with the cat gone, the birds
began to take an interest in Thomas. After all,
some of them were accustomed to eat creatures
of his size by the beakful. Spiders too were a
problem for him, and when it rained in the
garden Thomas frequently had to swim back to
the house.

Thomas was now the smallest person that
had ever lived and he was becoming famous for
it. His photograph and measurements appeared
in all the newspapers. The Mayor of the town
made a speech about him. The Duchess of Old
Hill arranged a grand ball in his honour.

Problems for Thomas

The Giant Baby

[One day the Hicks family find a giant baby on their doorstep. The news soon spreads …]
On Monday morning at seven o'clock the phone rang; Alice answered it. It was the reporter from the local paper wanting another interview. At twenty-past seven it rang again, this time a reporter from a national paper. By eight o'clock, three other reporters had phoned and a woman from the BBC.

During this time the giant baby had yelled for his breakfast, had his nappy changed, been heaved into his chair and eaten his breakfast. He had also discovered the game of dropping spoons on the floor. Alice (principal retriever) was supposed to be getting ready for school.

'Come on, get a move on,' said her mum.

'Do I have to?' 'Yes.'

[Soon a radio reporter arrives. The giant baby grabs his microphone and won't let go. . .]
Having briefly sucked the microphone, the baby gave a yell of satisfaction and banged it on the table. This had the effect of smashing a butter dish and deafening the poor sound engineer out in the van. Eventually, the giant baby was persuaded to give up his treasure. Mrs Hicks tempted him with a rolling pin and instantly regretted it. How were they going to get *that* off him?

Questions

1 | How is Baby Brick different from her parents?
2 | Why do Thomas and the giant baby become famous?
3 | What are some of the problems about being too big or too small?
4 | Are there any things about these stories that would help you to guess that they were by the same author?